RAMBLINGS FROM A SOUL

Peggy Woods

BALBOA.
PRESS

A DIVISION OF HAY HOUSE

Balboa Press books may be ordered through booksellers or by contacting:

Balboa Press
A Division of Hay House
1663 Liberty Drive
Bloomington, IN 47403
www.balboapress.com
1-(877) 407-4847

Because of the dynamic nature of the Internet, any web addresses or links contained in this book may have changed since publication and may no longer be valid. The views expressed in this work are solely those of the author and do not necessarily reflect the views of the publisher, and the publisher hereby disclaims any responsibility for them.

The author of this book does not dispense medical advice or prescribe the use of any technique as a form of treatment for physical, emotional, or medical problems without the advice of a physician, either directly or indirectly. The intent of the author is only to offer information of a general nature to help you in your quest for emotional and spiritual well-being. In the event you use any of the information in this book for yourself, which is your constitutional right, the author and the publisher assume no responsibility for your actions.

Any people depicted in stock imagery provided by Thinkstock are models, and such images are being used for illustrative purposes only.
Certain stock imagery © Thinkstock.

ISBN: 978-1-4525-3240-0 (sc)
ISBN: 978-1-4525-3241-7 (e)

Printed in the United States of America

Balboa Press rev. date: 7/28/2011

CONTENTS

DEDICATION

I dedicate this book first to my darlings, Rick and Will, for their constant love and support. I also dedicate it to my amazing "Wednesday night ladies", all of them, for allowing me to grow and become strong enough to take this step. To my NJ duo I express sincere thanks for letting me know others understand my words. My final dedication is to my Mama, who planted the seed that has finally seen the sun.

FOREWORD

My writings are an attempt to flip a switch,
turn on a light or gently tap you on the shoulder.
They are an attempt to suddenly make some things so clear
or lose their weight or pain altogether for the reader.
It is like writing a letter to get something out
and in "speaking" the words,
finally hearing what they actually say and mean.
Journaling these dreams and thoughts were my effort
to figure out what they were saying
or offer a perception not previously explored.
This book, I feel, is an opportunity to explore
by "holding the words in one's hand"
and seeing what they elicit from an individual.
It is an opportunity to revisit life;
a chance to make sense of something
made up of bits and pieces by laying
the whole scenario out to be digested.
I find that this outpouring is often not meant
to be consumed again immediately,
but at some future time
when the words may speak back differently
and paint a better picture of where I'm going.
It is my hope to mentally communicate on a blameless plain
with a fresh eye and perhaps an unclouded mind.
Often discoveries made change the landscape
of life or the direction of its path.

PEACE

Soul searching, us searching for it or it searching for us.
Does it really matter as long as the connection occurs and grows?
Sink deep into it, share wholly of it, belong to each other.
That is the salvation mankind needs to seek.
Be at peace with oneself.
That peace will seep into the cracks and crevices of other people's armor.
Someday we will shed that armor for something more glorifying of the soul-spirit.

Many are trying to catch the elusive scent and feel of peace,
feeling it just awakening in them, around them.
It can be hard to recognize something you have never truly encountered,
something of a shape, form, and substance unknown to you.
Believing that it is real may be the hardest part of all.

Represented in so many disguises, which one is real,
which one do you reach out to grasp to your soul?
It is only self-definable, self-reliable and self-propagated.
The attraction of it growing within you,
it is what draws others to believe
they too might come to know it.
Lead them not, for their path to peace is not the one you are walking.

Peace is as individual as the soul, indefinable to any other soul.
Yet when we each find that path the walls will come down,
the skies will lift up,
we will finally see that we are truly one entity.
Like a quaking grove of aspens interconnected in our creation,
stretching to join arms as the beautiful creatures we are
upon the earth.

Believe that the paths of peace are being uncovered, brushed off,
relieved of the overgrowth of weeds and thorns,
finally appearing in the sunlight of angels' eyes looking upon us.

Peace, peace, peace, even a beautiful word to say,
the final sound escaping, traveling into the distance,
traveling towards the soul.
Look for your peace,
clothe yourself with it,
let it light your way.
That light will shine bright enough for all someday.

GOD GAVE US NATURE

God gave us nature to help us understand
how credible the incredibly awesome can be:
an orchid, a spider web, the true display of oneness—water.
Flowing, shaping, nourishing everything we need, be or have.

COME THIS WAY

Kindness, humility, strength and hope—
traits of the good, not the wealthy?
Ah, that's where you are wrong, it can be both worlds.
To change this world will require wealth,
to change it for the better will require all of the other ingredients combined.
Excess and audaciousness, wanton disregard for resources,
both manmade and natural, belie the image of the wealthy.
Any image can be altered, revised, refined.
A slow transition to the other end of the scale
to help keep us in balance.

Balance, life, liberty and the pursuit of health and happiness
could become the revitalized "American dream."
The dream is now covered with ashes and gases,
the dream some never even heard of.
Too many mantras leading us in the wrong direction:
how does it feel to want,
life is not fair,
people like us don't deserve that kind of life,
the rich get richer and the poor get screwed.

What will it take to erase those mantras,
replace them with something phrased by hope and faith of whatever kind?
No need to wipe out a generation killing each other,
grasping for what someone else has
as if there is not enough for all.

We each earn our rewards,
some we deserve and some we can't seem to talk ourselves out of.
Is it possible to trudge our way down
to the innermost shrine inside of ourselves,
use the key, thought lost and long rusted,
crack the portal and allow our light to seep out?
That inner warmth is often a surprise,
unrecognizable and foreign
to our normal bag of emotions and attitudes.
Feels like a slip but strangely enough it feels good.

Was it real, how do we get it back?
Can it possibly be real and of substance?
Don't tempt fate or rock the pirogue,
that wisp of joy or peace or relief may never return.
It can only return if we revisit it, befriend it, nourish it
till it is too large to occupy that shrine-cum-prison within us.
Filling other spaces and seeping into pictures in our minds
and waves in our emotions.

Breathe in hopefully, breathe out glowingly.
Let that light shine before you,
light your way across the darkness,
help you find the outer portal that opens to shine on others.
Join their glow, shine as one,
we will grow stronger.
Seek the shimmer you glimpse haloing another being.
Follow the hope to outshine the sun,
the galaxy, the universe.
We have bottled enough experiences
from all realms in the darkness,
let us explore the unending realm in the light.
Come this way...

AGE OF CHANGE

Here, here at last, the tide does turn,
heads raise upwards.
Strength, hope and faith flow back through our veins
as if through long-empty caverns.
We come to pass the scepter to a new age,
an age of reason, there really wasn't one before.
An age of change, a different kind of change than allowed before.

We should have been wiser, we should not have judged.
We should have opened our eyes, ears and souls to find the spirit
alive in all peoples throughout this kind "rock" of ours.
We need to blend in, blend with,
become part of creation in the deepest sense of the word.

The pieces have fallen together,
the way is laid clear,
there are others like us that hold intangibles dear.
Oh the throng of joyful fellowship that will move toward a new horizon,
oh the surge of joy that will fill the voids we have allowed along the way.
Fill it with joy, hope and love above all.

SURROUNDINGS

Who else haunts the woods behind my dwelling place
whom I cannot reach out to.
Who walks on soft sounds and makes their path unknown to me.
Leave some traces, that I may find your mark
and read its story and learn its song and prayer.
Let me join as the one that we are meant to be.
Let my heart leap with joy
to join the family of souls that are mine and thine.

We share so much and so little of ourselves.
We must valiantly try to come out into the night
and play each other's songs.
Play our harps and hearts with gentle hands and soulful eyes.
Look out over the gathering of angels
and sense the heavenly presence filling the space.

DREAM

Rise above the earth bonds and make the leap to reach your dreams.
Dream, dream big, dream softly, dream sweetly,
dream safely, dream wildly, but do dream.
Never stop dreaming, dream your world into existence
and dream yourself out of your cave, your self-dug tunnel.
Be the spirit, fly the sky, soar the clouds,
move beyond the binding strains of the melody that brings you down.
Bring yourself above, below, inside, between
but bring yourself always into that good night.

BE WITH US

Good night, adieu,
we live to overcome this space and time
and spread our spirits wide and free.
Be gone from the dark, dear angels;
let the light shine forth among all.
We beseech thee to hear our cry,
answer our plea for grace and prayer.
Dear one, comfort us and offer your cloak to rest our head,
protect our souls from our own devised damnation.
Be with us spirit, be with us all, ye children of God,
as part of one another,
as part of the peace that coexists,
surrounding us.

WHAT WILL BE

Where is the courage that could dwell within?
Is it lost or does it hide?
Perhaps it is not courage but bravado,
not confidence but wishing,
not talent, but a loss of, from past lives.
Where is the wellspring within my soul
that can let flow all these things?
All these hopes and dreams, wishes and aspirations.
Am I a falsehood, be I not the one I wish,
am I a mirage of that which I wish to be?

Slow down, seek inside, find credit and credence and faith.
Believe in yourself—no one knows you quite as well,
no one gets inside your heart and head
to find the true spirit residing there.
What standards need I meet?
None but my own, and I build them so high
I cannot overcome them.
I am faint of heart, weak of soul,
if I behest my own self of all that I desire.
Make friends, make amends, coax, cajole;
kindness and heart reach further than staffs and prods.
Lead me to water and let me craft a fountain,
show me the world and let me give birth to a dream.
Why do I hold myself captive and let misery rein free?
Snap myself up and change what is into what should be,
what will be.

AS ONE

Faith in all, trust in all, be with all together.
The load will be carried,
the fight will be won, the honor restored.
The way to spend the whole together is mixed within.
One must not look out alone
but with the eyes of the whole body.
This shall be its answer and its salvation.
Be as one, feel as one, think as one and move as one.
Feel the flow of energy through all
and know it shall carry you too
and replenish your spirit anew.

We make our paths follow such bumpy roads
and we need not traverse them alone
but as a whole, as one being.
Know that we intercept one another's paths
as ripples cover the surface of the water.
All is whole beneath it and passes around,
mingles with all that is there.
Settle down once again to surface tension
but not tension in the normal sense,
more a field of energy that binds us together—
billions of tiny energy pieces that fly around each other,
passing safely through the fields, never taking the same way twice.
Always new, always searching for other connections, other purposes.
Help us to find our purpose and connect.
Give us strength, give us guidance,
let us see the light and pass the way of truth.
Bless us each and everyone,
in your glorious sight,
with your glorious light.

LIFE IN NO TIME AT ALL

Boy, it's hard to hold onto a perspective.
Swaying from a position of abject fear
to glimmering hope has a way of throwing one off balance.
Not that one is any more off or out of balance
than the rest of mankind,
or so one likes to think.
One book leaves you resting assured
that focusing on what you want in life
will make it appear.
Reality is the only one who has a clue
what the real rap is all about.

For some, it depends on the digit
in front of the decimal in the checkbook.
A minimum of three is the only thing
that leaves them breathing;
anything less might as well be behind the dot.
Money disappears faster and with more agility
than ice cream melts in a blast furnace.

Can you fool yourself
into thinking that something will keep filling up the void;
that it will never pass below those magic spaces.
Earnestly try to believe that "if God feeds the birds,
and clothes the lilies of the field..."

INTELLIGENCE INBORN

To grow in belief,
to grow in wealth,
tangible and intangible.
The change it can bring is sometimes overwhelming.
The calm and logical approach to change of lifestyles is essential.
Do not go forward with fear and trepidation.
Step boldly into the future, confident to meet the challenge,
rise to the level of intelligence inborn.
The inherent aptitude of one's own convictions and beliefs,
the flowering of one's dawning reality,
drenched in freeness of spirit and strength of soul.
Come along for the ride.
It will be unlike any traveled before.

ITS OWN SIGNATURE

Each path has its own signature.
Sign it slowly and with great love and deep gratitude.
Spread the width of the path
so it encourages and enfolds many along the way.
Many, so that each bring their own path,
so that the future might be taken into a new direction.

CRITICAL MASS

Critical mass,
a concept that quantum physics has brought to the fore,
let us be the ones that define it.
Love of life, freedom of spirit,
respect for all sways together in the wave of the future.
Find a spot along the path, among loved ones,
encouraging all to move toward
the individual lights we all are searching for.
The infinity of space and the finite scope of our part
must become clear to all for the hope of a true future.
Let us reflect on the speck that we are.
Take in the whole essence
of that finite aspect that we play in the universe.

LET IT OUT

Passion, fuel for the fire,
a purpose given and not withdrawn.
Life should be all-consuming, all-encompassing, all-definable.
We needn't search further for our purpose,
it lies within, unveil the sculpture of it,
the beauty of it, let light in for the world to see.
You are the creator and outlet for your passion.
Don't trap it inside as a genie in a bottle.
Rub it, polish it, admire it.
It need not be hidden as if someone might steal it.

All those genies in bottles meandering
across the face of this planet
in search of their own way out.
Imagine a world where they all were free.
Believe that things could be amazing, stupendous,
out of touch with mere mortal rationalization.
We are creators, gifted by God, led by our own inner spirit,
the hopeful product of our purpose here on this plane.

Find the source, the magic resonance
that will pop all those bottles open and let the genies out.
See what they can do. What harm can there be
for each creation to create its purpose,
let shine its glory, follow its dream?
Watch each move freely between its brothers and sisters,
mingling in and out, up and down, side to side.
Let there be no bottle unopened, let them all out.
Free them, free us, free eternity.
Let the powers and the beauty and the cascades
of all creations flow like a waterfall
feeding the river of life with its fullness and freshness.
Set them free, the incredible, and finally find them credible.
Believe in more than three wishes; believe in a forever chain
linked in many fashions that crisscross the horizon
as far as our God's eye can see.
Let it out.

ROOTS FOR YOUR SPIRIT

Grow my child, spread your wings.
Stumble and fall, pick yourself up again.
Try on grown things, find just your fit.
Mind that your gift has but one round this time.
Guard it with love and earn it with peace.
I feel your strength and know your heart is good.
Fly my child, upward and onward.
Cherish the time you have and be open to all you can learn.
My gift to you is roots for your spirit,
love for your soul.
Be guided by your light.
I love you, my child.

ENVISION THE REALM

Allow, release, feel unafraid.
Seek no reason, just be in the moment,
the joy of the moment that you can create.
You are in charge of that moment.
You are the structural, esthetic, mechanical
architect of that moment. Spend it how you choose.
As they say, "a thimble or a mansion" matters not
but to you the creator. Each of us has that creator inside.

Formal introductions should not be necessary,
but sometimes maps are...
Finding our creator, nurturing and nourishing it,
a bit similar to parenthood.
It comes with no manuals, no rights or wrongs, just our way;
For the good of ourselves or the detriment.
Leave it to the judge,
the emotional guidance system we all came with.
We need to but fine-tune our radar, our energy fields,
to open up the vast universe available.
Finding the control knobs are the key,
for there are no tangible dials;
they are internal and eternal.
It would be wonderful if we could hit the default switch
and assume the program we came down for,
but even that was not fully fleshed out shall we say.
We recommend meditation,
the single opportunity to quiet the mind
and move about free of restraints
and inhibitions, supposedly.
Even that takes learning.
It is all there is and all we seek to continue
learning our way back to the other side.
Envision a place full of sun,
windows large and warm with the brightness of day,
safe and secure with the darkness of the night.
A place to see the stars, as many as possible, as far as possible.
A door that opens wide for friends to come through.
A piece of paradise that stimulates the creator in each.

Oh the things we could create
if we only knew how to get out of our own way.
ABCs, 123s, building blocks, stumbling blocks,
opportunities to achieve something greater
than the individual pieces of our lives.
It really is all about the beyond.
We get drawn into the tangibles, the mundane,
the repetitiveness of our bogged-down lives.
Move past that, into another realm.
Envision the realm.

RITE OF PASSAGE

How do we reach each other?
Through smiles and waves, words and expressions.
Our world has so many means of communication,
yet do we really accomplish anything
but barely scratching the surface of what needs to be shared?

A favorite expression which is merely a damnation is
"rite of passage,"
An interesting way of saying that if we had to endure it
so do all the coming generations.
Yes, people learn best through their own experience
but there are some trials that could merit at least preparation
if not total avoidance.

If some of us would have the presence of mind and an open heart
to realize the possible value to mankind
to change or eliminate some of those rites.
True, these rites vary from age to age, culture to culture;
but some forethought could
possibly change mankind's direction all together.
Surely some of the brighter minds existing on this planet
could devise more rewarding, productive
and effective methods of teaching.

Is it not possible to share
with the younger generations
the information or insight to avoid
or overcome some of the rites that many of us have
needed therapy to help erase or put in perspective.
What if we taught some form of psychology to our younger generations
beginning at the very earliest ages
so that they might actually be able to survive,
perhaps even excel through the "growing-up" years.

Most often a parent or guardian would wish to impart some knowledge
that might alleviate a shard of pain and anguish experienced during that time.
Yet with our current philosophy and attitude
having that information coming only from them carries no value,
in fact is often disdained.
But when heard from other sources,
possibly introduced and activated in education,
these same ground rules could assume an entirely different worth.
How many collective sighs of relief have we exhaled
when our child finally comes to that reality because "so and so said blah."
The hard part being not to say, "I told you so already."
Merely rejoicing in the fact that the concept
has been received and possibly put into play.
How quickly could mankind discard so many things.
Imagine.

DO NOT BE AFRAID

So what does one write about?
One's self, mankind, humankind, spirit kind.
Thoughts and phrases that flit through one's head.
Words that arise from the bogs of one's mind
to shape into messages for everyone and no one.
Don't be afraid to do it. You're not hurting anyone
and you are assuaging your soul and spirit.

Let it foam and dribble or let it froth and tumble to the paper,
off into the twilight of the written word.
This may open up your pathway,
help you find it and manifest it.
Wherever, whatever and whichever way it is destined to lead.
At least it is an opening, a portal
that may eventually shed some light on your true path.

Find your way, find your center,
find your peace so that it fills you
and encompasses your world.
Let it lead you, wind its path through hollow
or canyons made from rock or concrete.
Do not diminish your purpose.
It has possibly been growing for generations.
Let it bear fruit, whether bruised and scarred,
puny and tasteless or plump and ripe.
Full of the sweetness of overflowing spirit calling to others,
clasping hand and melding souls.
Let it breathe, let it live; do not be afraid...

WHERE DO THE WORDS COME FROM

Where do the words come from, really unbidden?
They slide into my head and back out on paper.
At times I'm not really sure what I said or why.
The topic chooses itself.
I never know what's coming next
or if it will be of any worth, even unto myself.

That is why for so long my words
lay hidden under illegible scrawl,
often so illegible even I could not
determine the word or phrase.
There is a secret flow of energy in each of us
that we oft seem unaware of
or allow out in the wrong direction.
Sometimes we fear reprisal, our own reprisal,
for having such thoughts, never mind letting them out.

Journaling is something finally recognized
as an outlet for many voices with many reasons.
How many of us ponder whether we would be committed
should we ever let another's eyes flow across the page,
much less ever let lips utter the verbiage.
There are those of us that cannot dam up the flow forever,
I believe none of us should.
Irregardless of what concoction we are laying loose upon the page
it has a place in our growth and our sanity
and possibly our own soul's journey.

Ink and paper, electronic pulses in a computer
reforming into a document,
who knows what worth it holds for the creator?
That is truly all that matters anyway.
The purpose it serves to its creator is the whole point.
We seek not bounty or acclaim,
we seek only to relinquish some of the jumble in our minds
to find a new place for it to dwell
and a new space be freed to fill again.

The words assume all sorts of roles,
weapons, hearts, tears, light,
the choice is in the mind of the emitter
determining whether the role
will ever be played out or tossed out.
Often times the release need only benefit the drafter,
providing the opportunity to cleanse
or replenish a need known only to them.
But do write it down, circuit it out into cyberspace
or burn it after to absolve or resolve the need to create it at all.

There are so many words, phrases and wishes in our heads,
troubling or fulfilling our heart. Allow yourself to make room for more.
More to heal with, more to love with
or more to leave behind to remember with.
Let it out and breathe free for a brief moment of release.
Then take up your pen, your sword,
your Cupid's arrow again and start anew.
You might find the path changing,
the darkness lightening, or the spirit growing.
It's all part of why we're here;
use it for each individual's necessity
and allow them to choose its fate.

Journal

IS THERE SOUND?

I know there is light and motion, is there sound?
Does the ethereal float with beautiful music or angels singing?
Are you greeted by the sound you find comfort in?
That cannot totally be, for you have left those sounds behind
in the voices of the ones you loved.

Now is not when you want to hear them,
sobbing or lamenting at your passage.
Maybe it will be memories of their voices,
the laughter, the first cry of your babies,
their first words, "I love you" from the one you loved.
Whatever they are I hope they will be blessed.

You will be welcomed back "home"
with open hearts and faces and voices
long missed but oft dreamt of.
Be at peace my darling, at peace,
and reveling in joy that you have arrived safely home
Now it is your turn to peer through the clouds
and join us in spirit as we beckon you to us.

I know our souls will join again
and plot and plan another journey through this plane,
to experience new and wonderful aspects
of the earthly realm we may have missed heretofore.
Oh my dearest, what shall we do this next time,
what roles will we play, joys we will experience,
and memories to make to evolve into our future souls.
Enjoy the sounds if you can,
let me hear a snippet.
I love you.

IT IS TIME

So it is time, finally, my dearest friend.
I promise to try to be brave, try to be calm.
I have plenty of time to remember things, plenty of time to cry.
It is your bon voyage party, one we never planned
but openly welcome now for your release.
We need no revisiting of the past months,
no recriminations of the pieces of the puzzle
that fell into place to bring us here.
We won't all embrace this trespass but it was your choice,
and those of us left standing behind must accept it,
if not graciously, at least gently,
for your burden was carried bravely and you need to move on.

Be our guide, our inspiration;
the patience and attitude you assumed
during this trial denotes your character
your demeanor, my darlin'.
"I have my good days and my bad days"
became your badge of courage.
We knew even the good days never quite measured up
but you shared so little of what you were going through.
You refused to allow others to carry the burden you bore,
you carried it calmly and painfully.
I wish I had been able to hear your times of screaming, crying,
thrashing and cursing, but I know that was not your way.

We both somehow knew this battle could not be won,
this enemy chased from the chambers
it had overtaken would not be allowed.
We had to relive the past again as Charlotte left
before she cuddled her grandbabies,
before she knew the man who would carry you
through all the trials and joys of life.
Your path follows hers, but why?
My heart and my head scream why.
Couldn't this have been different,
someday I will ask the explanation for the biding of time
and exiting before we reached a culmination of dreams
in the soft breath of your grandchild's sleeping visage.

I hope someday that you will bring me through the clouds into the sun,
the light that illuminates the path we trod wherever we plotted.
I know it is now time.
The main use of tears at present is to ease our own ache,
soothe our own heart and bridge our own fear of this final passage.
We let you go, my love.
Go with God and peace and our love.

COLORS OF A PALATE

The remaining green blades quiver in the breeze
among the brown stiff stalks of the dying grasses.
Fall is nearing its end and winter blowing upon us
as if to prepare us to hunker down and hibernate.
Instead we forge on through snow,
slush and ice with our faces wrapped in scarves,
our eyes filled with tears, fighting off the frigid air.

Down south they could have ice cream
on Christmas Day or frost at Easter.
Weather and mother nature make sure
that guesstimates and predictions
are beyond mortal reason and outside any control.
Oft times she sets us up for a slam dunk
just to prove we may never be in charge.
How presumptuous are we to assume such is ever a possibility?

This did not begin about the weather,
it began staring at the repetitious patterns
where the breeze stirred those grasses.
How many grasses have stirred; short, tall,
all the colors of the palate that nature
endows her makeup artists with.
The grasses are the defining image
of the scenery as it changes through life.
The bountiful grasses in the yards in south Louisiana,
the tall graceful, colorful grasses of the road and hillside in Colorado.
Interspersed with the wild grasses and
bountifully beautiful flowers of the Texas landscape.

The palate we so seek to replicate
yet seldom seem to imitate to quite the beauty of nature herself.
We are eager painters and designers that at times
facetiously believe we can possibly surpass the real thing.
What fools we are, how she laughs...

NEW WORDS

Glue, duct tape, band aids, chewing gum,
the attempts we make to mend or hold our lives together.
Various stages of repair, replacement, known as rehab or divorce
to a whole alphabet soup of other words
that have become too commonplace in our vocabulary.
Somewhere along the line faith, hope, trust,
promises and commitments were redefined.
The definitions are the holes in the fabric of our current society.

Bring something up, anything
and someone will either want to change it or rename it.
How many new words, words of substance and impact,
have we added to our dictionaries in the last fifty years?
How many words of attitude and bias and division have been enfolded
or outright replaced, words once uttered with a pure and simple purpose.
What about all the "special" words, the "PC" words.

Would it be in our better interest to strive
to create new words for new visions,
new accomplishments, new milestones?
New strides that garner a better existence,
a brighter future, an ascension of our state of essence and soul.
But then words have most often been incomplete
to express the emotional evolution of man and nature.
No word replaces the smell, feel or touch of the actual reality.
They are mere attempts to bridge the chasm
between what we say and what we feel.

Some day perhaps we will bridge that gap
and travel beyond the need for taunts and teeth
to convey the inner expressions of our soul.
Words are sounds uttered with individual judgments
choosing the pattern of the phrase.
Some day may we all be able to see instead of say "I love you."

EXCHANGE

The sun feels good, warming up my back,
chasing the chill from my hands.
The chill comes from the conditioned air
inside my daytime penitentiary.
I am not penitent when I dwell there,
merely tolerant of my need to in order to have exchange
for the things I choose to fill my world.

Exchange for a home and vehicles, food and threads to clothe me.
Would I strive for exchange for those things intangible,
the balance would be different.
My exchanges could never buy enough freedom,
time for reflection, moments of peace.
Some dream of a future where the exchange
will be more balanced, more benevolent, more fruitful.
A dream of exchange for the purpose
your soul chose to incarnate for.
A reality created with the giving of oneself
and the rewarding of that giving by others whom it benefits.

You wonder whether that could be possible;
a world that exists solely for joy and fulfillment,
not giving way to greed or excess.
A true weighing of the individual value of each soul's purpose,
diving in the direction that would lead us to.
We never seem to be able to wholly depart
from some inner fear of lack, of want.
Could we ever trust to that level
that someone would not overstep their purpose and tread on others,
leaving lives bereft and hopeless.
Somewhere, someday there will be a joining of the souls,
a melding of the spirits creating a realm of heaven on earth.
For now we must continue our exchanges
and not let go of our dreams.

WHAT GRIEF IS NOT

How does one judge another's passage through grief.
It cannot and should not be done.
We each hold a different place in our hearts
for those we have lost.
We each have a different measure and threshold
for the emotion that accompanies that loss.
Unless we realize how self-involved our grief is
we should not examine another's.

Those who have passed on leave no demands behind.
They do not ask nor expect payment be made to their memory.
Their souls realize, possibly for the first time,
the real value they held here on earth.
Yet they need no display or demonstration to evaluate that worth.
They can clearly feel it in the hearts of those they left behind.
They do not ask that we exile ourselves from the living,
instead they hope that their passing may instill a greater realization;
how precious every second of our earthly life should be.

Grief is not something to be examined and graded.
It is not something that punches a time clock or marks off a calendar.
It is the road our individual hearts and souls must travel
to hopefully find peace in the future and cherish memories of the past.
Not to drown in our own selfish loss
but to revel in the gift of having had the departed once be a part of our lives.

Everyone's needs are different, as is everyone's courage, faith and strength.
Banish not those you may judge weaker or less deserving.
We all are allowed a stake in that soul's journey here with us.
Deal only with yourself and your soul and your faith on the passing of another.

THE TIES THAT BIND

Yes, the ties that bind are often painful.
They sometimes lead to places we do not care to explore.
But somewhere, somehow, we choose those ties
and the length of their strings.
We still sought to come forth in this place,
to follow those paths wherever they took us.
Each spirit carries within it a gift.
We need to partake of that gift during this time and space.
Those that have chosen to stretch those ties
to the ethereal boundaries do so
with a whole heart, remembering
what purposes lie in their travel.

They do not wish for us to wonder
what they would have done or been
for they had already met their goal in that sense.
To be able to accept such beauty and brightness
for however long a time
is one of our greatest and hardest lessons.
We are a mere blip of time and space.
Marvel at all that we manage to fit
into that framework however big.
Come to face the reality
of what our job remains while we are here.

So many comings and goings, joys and sorrows,
all colors in a still life that we paint moment by moment.
We need to give up our angst and our possession
of the spirits we touch who fly free.
We need to find a way to absorb their strength
and remember the beauty of each of their entities.
We are so earthbound and those ties
that bind us here can chafe and wear upon us.
These other spirits make the travel easier to bear.

Fear not, though, that someone will begin to mend your heart
and bring you forward enough to look back on the light and beauty
with love and gratitude for the face they painted on your journey.
Each of us is able to choose, pray that your choice
will honor the tie you can no longer bind to you in this realm.

TIME'S MEASURE

Time in a bottle, life under glass,
seeing inside and out, over, under and through.
Why are we concerned with time?
What does it have to do with life?
It is only on the face of a clock
not the gaze in the eye of a loved one.
It does not measure emotion,
only whether it is dark or light out when we experience it.

They say it really has no measure in reality.
It has no value in soulfulness and empathy.
Time stretches out in all directions
as if a paintbrush crazed
with the desire to experience all the space
it can cover in the blink of an eye.
We never know when we are really here or there,
we never know when there is right or wrong.

Time is simply in the mind of the beholder
and the sigh of the breath we take to continue living.
Where does it begin and end,
is it so simple as the tick of a clock,
one less minute of our time in this realm exists.
They say our life here is but the blink of an eye.
How can that be when we are trapped in it in pain or suffering or loss.

Time seems forever and so barren
when we have lost someone we love.
It seems so minute by minute, day by day.
The trick is to not get trapped by that scenario,
not to focus on the overwhelming amazement
of existing for any minute, any day.
It is the present, as they say pre-sent—
but how do we seem to know what to
do with it and when we don't
how does it seem to drag on forever.

What is a moment like to someone with Alzheimer sitting in a wheelchair,
passing the day staring at things that make no more sense?
Does it lift when that time is instead spent staring at a tree
with its leaves rippling in the breeze or a bird fluffing its feathers?
How long is time to a baby that has just begun this trek?
Sleep, eat, and so on until the brain begins to click
in greater links of sense.

Time must be something we invented
to pass and measure where we are.
Count the days you have been alive;
at fifty-eight it is over 21,000 and something.
How were those days spent?
How many wasted partially or wholly?
How many invested in others and memories
that will help carry us through the times in that wheelchair.
Believe in the present only,
for the next second does not exist until you pass through it;
take pause to consider how you value it.
Take pause to absorb all of the around you stuff
that exists seen or unseen.
Weigh it and measure how you use it,
believe that you will look back at it some time to relive it gladly.

WRAPPED IN YOUR ARMS

Oh to be held in your arms again, to feel your warmth, your life,
your breath gently whispering past my ear.
How good that would feel again.
How much I miss those hugs hello and goodbye.
Can we even begin to grasp
the fragility of a life that we touch and love.
To know someone so deeply or so long and lose them forever,
or until only our souls can touch again.

I hope there are hugs in heaven,
the cuddle of someone loved who loves you back.
The fit of each other together whether just friends or loved ones.
To smell that sole identifying mixture of scents that make up their private brew.
To feel the swell of your own heart for that brief time
where it is safe to wrap them in your arms.
The feel of their hair or skin or mustache on your neck.
The tease of their lips on your cheek.
Oh to be held in your arms one more time,
to lay my head upon your shoulder,
your breast, and listen to the heartbeat now stilled.
Give of yourself in ways that cannot be measured
but by purely wrapping your arms about another in friendship or love.
Let that feeling linger, waiting in your memory
to revisit and draw strength from.
Never miss that opportunity to hold them in your arms.

WE ARE WHAT WE ARE

Why do we think of ourselves that way,
with guilt or disdain, disappointment or anger.
We are what we are in this moment in time.
Changing it in the next is up to us.
Never visit self loathing or pity,
never dwell with disappointment and downheartedness.
Find the path to the next moment
of treasure and discovery of what we really are,
who we really can be.
The wake of a boat lies behind it,
the azure blue water lies before it to be crossed
with a soaring joy that can only come in the innocence
of moving forward with hope and promise.
Don't bury yourself before your time.
Look to the sky and the heavens
and in another person's eyes to see what can be,
witness that promise of a future on a new journey.
Where we go from here depends on
what vision we can affix in front of us
to dream towards, strive for, believe in.
Give yourself a chance, open up your heart to yourself,
meld it into your mind to revitalize your future.
Feel the difference in your body,
embrace the difference this will bring to your soul.
Imagine, close your eyes,
feel with your senses and change your direction.

NO BEFORE, NO AFTER

Lost loves, old loves, true loves;
how does one know the difference?
What makes the difference?
Love finds its own way through space and time;
we aid it by opening our eyes and our hearts,
by allowing different things to make the difference.

Is it looks or smile or heart or mind that is the key;
a combination thereof or a need fulfilled.
Love is so simple in its basic form.
Lasting love is the one that begs to differ,
the one that requires investment of time and heart.
Investment of soul and spirit override the minor detours.

Even lasting love can have bumps in the road,
periods of desolation found in the soul or heart of one;
spirit dictates the volume and depth of that love.
Feeling overcomes those periods and you awaken again
that curl in your tummy when your love comes into view.

Day by day you build the strength of love,
week by week you build the countenance of it.
Time becomes irrelevant when it is lasting,
there becomes no before, no after, only now
and now keeps going on and on and on.

Curiosity peeks our interest as time passes.
What if this or what if that?
But then one stops and realizes that it is all in passing.
The truth lies in the melding of two souls that love binds.
That is where the *this* and *that* end and the *forever* remains.

Love comes in so many forms, forms to fit everything,
to fit every need, but true and lasting love fills the soul.
It keeps the flow of life and energy channeling
between two hands and one whole heart.

FILL IN THE BLANKS

Who was that person, what role did they play?
One of development or learning;
one of anguish and pain.
One of thrill and the rush of emotion and fever?
What remains of their contribution to who we are now?

All these things come together to produce us now,
without them we would have gone in another direction perhaps.
We may have missed a part of the real us.
It all has a purpose, we just need to fill in the blanks,
let the chips fall the way they did, and focus on tomorrow's path.

We have each added to the other's lives in immeasurable ways.
No need to take that measurement, only know that it filled a blank.
There are no blanks in the past, only the ones to fill in the future.

MY CHILD

He's home already, he's mine already.
No waiting for phone calls or airplanes,
only waiting for his sleepy head to wake up.
Wait for the sight of that face that you have watched change,
absorb the reality of his presence here with you.

The web was woven well and strong,
dropped stitches or broken threads
matter not in the final pattern.
They are all part of the beauty of the piece,
the family knows that it will never wear out
and never fray.

BIND THESE WOUNDS

The Lord giveth and the Lord taketh away...
Why, we ask, why? We search our souls begging for a reason.
Trust and faith are not always comfort enough
and seldom dry the tears that follow when he taketh.

They say each entry into existence of a soul
has a reason even if the soul never greets the light of day.
Its reason, its purpose remains
on the other side as part of some eternal plan.
What part of that plan and why or how
will not be privy to us until we cross.
Even the briefest will stop the hearts involved
and stir up emotions, grief and often anger,
that we must wade our way through.
Biding time until the pain eases
or the memories soften is the hardest part of the journey.
That we make this journey accompanied
by this soul is sometimes hard to believe,
even harder to find comfort in,
especially when we never got to know them
or see their face to give a picture to the memory.
There is little solace in the loss of one unborn,
little comfort in the hope and belief that this way is best.

Seek not to judge the wisdom or the love of our Lord,
he abides within us all;
he never varies from his love for each of us, born or unborn.
The message may remain a secret, the angst may remain a scar,
but the love remains undeniable and indefinable.
Seek your comfort in his arms; there is no greater comfort
though we may fight the embrace at first in pain and anger.
The embrace remains, lean back into it, have faith in it,
know that embrace will always catch you when you fall
no matter the fire vented upon it from your heart and mind.
The soul can help us find peace,
peace within the arms of something greater
and more encompassing that we can conceive.

Let go, let God, let love bind these wounds.
Let spiritual essence refuel our souls
and guide our spirits on the remaining journey.

TASTE THE LIFE

I am winning, I am really winning—
I think I can trust me and love me
and feel other people react somewhere near the same.
It's been a while since I've been brave enough
to take pen to paper.
Too much stuff in my head.
Such a plethora of new visions to select for my own;
they are my own.
I intend to be wealthy, I intend to share that wealth
and love and time and compassion.
I will travel to the places that have long lived in my mind
and taste the life we were taught is not ours to hope for.
I believe in myself and I believe in my beliefs—

DREAM THE RAINBOW'S END

Life is about choices.
You make them and break them,
collect them and reject them.
It is like the whirling sides of a coin.
You cannot tell if heads or tails
will be the last face before going over the edge.
It is only a matter of time and time inevitably waits for no one.
Learning to see the present as a gift and not rush its passing
to get on with life is a hard lesson to learn and master.
Looking around to see who is still there,
who could serve to keep you in touch with your path.
It might even shorten the trail to the rainbow's end.
We all would and should like to seek that end.
So many of us have it ripped out of our hearts
before we even realized it was there.
The glimpses of future dreams
turned reality are more frequent and more vivid,
as much like déjà vu as something from the past.
Our present is our step in the direction of our future.
Look up and face the whole picture,
stop looking down to only see the cobblestones.
We make our own bed but lie in another when we dream.
Dream the bed you wish to be in and visualize it into reality.
We create our auras, our egos;
our souls were born before us and know the real us.
We have such things inside us as we need to carry us through.
It is our heritage to move on;
it takes boldness to choose new paths and hopes.
We can only go where no one has gone before
if we can imagine the way.
We must release ourselves to the spirit
and regain our soul-searching
till we find ourselves and settle into our present,
safe in this new dimension.

THE MAKER OF ME

I am not the maker of things that I wish to be,
at least not yet.
The freedom of my soul has not found its door yet
or the strength to grasp and open it.
My own self has yet to grow strong
and re-emerge with the beginnings
that were stifled long ago.
There is so much inside that must come out.
The softness of sighing and loving,
the pain and hurt of crying and loneliness,
the warm beauty and fullness inside
that grows with the knowledge of one's own worth.
How beautiful we are when we realize
who we are and what we can be.
I have such a long way to go
but yet I have come such a far piece already.
I may never see the realization of my soul
but the idea that it is being born again
excites me beyond the basic existence.
I can no longer look in the corner and find no way out.
I have turned around and placed my back against the corner
to use it as my strength, not my limitation.
I can reach out before me now
and touch the edges of my dreams
and feel their fineness
and their shapes beginning to form.
I do have a long way to go but I have a strong back
and a strong mind
and the seed of courage nurturing within me.
Thank you to myself.

RIPPLES

This is the real me.
I am now in dimension.
I have thoughts that ripple outward,
created by listening inward.
It is really so simple.
Don't frown, don't scowl, and don't judge.
Do smile, do reflect, and do love.
I can finally hear my own voice,
brave enough to speak.
Talk softly and carry an open heart.
I have forgotten her.
Her image fades into an old photograph.
She is another person from another lifetime.
I am sure she has shaped me in some fashion.
Maybe I am the person she would have become.
Too many lifetimes stood in her way.
Too many cooks diluted her creation.
How is she related to me?
She is the flat face in the photograph.
I am the living dimension having escaped the past.

LISTEN

Why me, we always say.
We should listen to what we say more often.
Say what we want to our inner ear, the soul.
Practice that peace we wish to hear and feel.
Know that somewhere it resides in all of us.
Let the force of love and the wish
for simple happiness be with each of us.
Allow it to overtake your hurried steps
and chase down your racing mind.
Let it settle into your heart, setting up hearth and home.
Welcome everyone into the warm, the safe, the free.

THE GARDEN

She meant well, we always say.
This followed with, "She didn't know any better,"
is her place in our souls.
When you grow up on the defensive
the best way you can play is by the rules you have learned.
She had no trophies of her own so she wore ours,
not realizing who they really belonged to.
In her mind's eye, she believed
that is what her teachings had reaped for her.
The harvest was bleak loneliness
with afore unknown love folded in.
The seed packet we were each born with
would have to be nourished by another.
It would be brought to fruit by tears
and other caregivers within the garden boundaries.
Her garden was empty,
ravaged by a will unrelenting to her unconscious soul.
She realized she had meant well,
but it was too late to water the garden.

SHE LOVED US

She loved us.
That's all we need to know.
She did quite well for never
having known a mother's love.
In her repertoire of maternal actions
and activities she excelled,
overcoming limitations both monetary and perceptual.
Three buses to make a trip to the park.
Deviled ham and crackers on the edge
of the goldfish pond.
Generosity of heart to let us
feed those costly crackers to the fish
enabling us to experience 'nature' in city form.

So many things no longer matter,
so many seeming wrongs scratched off the list.
Actually to instead laud the attempts
at providing what was lacking ,
both materially and experientially.
Memories that I have now set free in my own life.
A long bus trip uptown to be able to experience
the interior of a house of grandeur,
something never expected to be our realm,
before it was torn down.
Nights spent on cold concrete steps fishing
for the rare catch of something edible.
The so desirable catch of time with her son
outweighed indulging him until 2 in the morning.

I perceived so many wrongs,
though some truly molded my character
in ways I would seek to change.
Most were totally irrelevant in the scheme of things,
compared against the reality of true abuse
that exists in the world today.
In the end the seed planted and nurtured
via her own inborn nature turned out be worthwhile.
A testament to her singular purpose in life
is the treasure of her children, grown and loved.

WHO WERE THEY

Who were they? They lived for seven decades each,
but could anyone say what they thought or felt?
No more to write about them,
no more to write about their sorrow for fear of drowning the future.
Realize they were the seed that fed our future.
Look out with hope upon this time and with direction.
Lead yourself on to your new destiny. Be happy...

A FINE WEB

All the colors of me and you joining together.
I am a part yet not a part from any other.
I am myself and you are my brother and sister.
We blend, we flow, we caress each atom
and carry it onto future generations.
What can we do to preserve this flow,
to make it whole and heal its wounds?
Where is the tie that binds yet lies buried
beneath remains that obscure it from view?
You are me and I am you.
Inseparable, insatiable, insurmountable when whole.
Oh to find that wholeness again, to find the rest of one's self
and wrench it back from the black sea of despair.
Eternal is the hope for us.
Internal lies the need for us.
External exists the part of us often hither and askew.
Gather them up and weave them together
to make a fine web to catch the spirit in.
Use the web to rescue the drowning soul from eternal separation.
Rejoice in the melding of these signs and symbols of our presence.
Keep them before us as a quest for the thirsting heart and soul.
Speak not of division and control, ruling and ruled;
Let the voice come of its own accord.
He knew what he did all along.
He felt no regret at being chosen the messenger
for the rewards were great though seeming small to the living.
Many have passed his same way and met a similar fate.
What we cannot comprehend, we eliminate.
Why do we see our birthright as a struggle to glean
the knowledge for the fruit of future generations?
Why do we not seek our future by racing wholeheartedly
up the path, sun shining in our faces?

NEW KNOTS

Can you feel the web between us?
The fine silk vibrating with energy and life.
Force flows from each of us intricately spinning this web.
We must learn more new stitches, more new knots.
Weave in gold and silver, faith and love.
Find the pattern that repairs
and returns us to our places side by side.
We are part of the single strand of humanity.
We cannot deny our connection and our obligations.
We are here and now we are taking the leap for faith.
We are being rewarded, being loved
and chosen to spread our love to others.
We share in our fortune and build new bridges to the future.
We have our chosen path and must clothe ourselves thusly
so as to make the trek to eternity.
Thank each of us for the role we play
as it broadens to encompass many lives.
We are the chosen and we will begin the future
and head in the direction of our destiny.
We love our new path, our new relationships,
our new home, our new extended family.
Thank you for the path you have laid before us
and the courage you give us to take it up.

OUR POCKETS ARE NEVER EMPTY

Spendthrift or extravagance.
Life finds its own value and rate of exchange.
Take the time and slow down, not take the money and run.
Seconds are the gold coins of existence
and minutes the savings bonds of our memories.
That picture imprinted in our brains, like George on a dollar bill,
has more value and credit than any plastic.
It is the tally of the times that add up to the sum of who we are.
Our pockets are never empty.
Hard cold coins and dirty paper dollars
don't fill the lining of our heart to keep us warm and comfortable.
They disappear as quickly as the days on the calendar.
Tear them off as they go and drop them in the trash.
The memories are eternal
and no amount of crumpling can change their image.
Choose the currency you save wisely and well.

METAMORPHOSIS

Thrust yourself into your future.
Find its outline and begin to pull the threads together.
Turn and gather the gifts and trappings to take with you.
Bundle in your precious cargo and make your journey light.
Carrying love and memories weigh nothing on the heart and soul.
Know that when you aim yourself,
you will follow as surely as the seed grows.
Place yourself in that dream and make it your reality.
Find the power to pull yourself above
the swirling, sucking depth and fly to freedom.
Wait to find your home among the clouds
between the earth and spirit.
Welcome all to your dwelling and relieve them of their bonds.
Meld all into one soul that will replenish the earth and sky.
Beauty, song, prayer and love
make a melody for transformation.
Metamorphosis
Beginning
Life
Eternity
Love

EBB AND FLOW

Life is too short for us to spend it judging every decision.
We need to stay in touch with our feelings,
seek our own level of peace and tranquility.
Let the ebb and flow of things ease our path.
If we are true to ourselves, then we will be at peace.
The highest thought, the grandest feeling, the deepest joy.
That is what tells us where we are and who we are.
Listen, feel and grow.
Life is so precious.
A smile, a hug, a laugh.

SAVE ME A PLACE

The time to let go is approaching.
We needn't fear it, but we certainly won't relish it.
It will give you relief and us a certain peace,
knowing you are beyond all that hurts
and all that clouds our own vision of the horizon.
Life never prompts us to make decisions based on our spirits.
It is the soul inside us that attempts to cling
to the path we've chosen to travel.

Neither you nor I find solace in this parting
but it must be for whatever part of the plan it is.
You will remember when you reach the haven of heaven.
I wish so that I could hold your hand until you arrive.
I know I can only send you off with love and prayers
and that age old request to let me know you have arrived safely.
I know I will feel you, hear you and be guarded over by you
for I have need of a great angel on the other side.

Know how hard it is for us to let go.
I cannot comprehend your earthly emotion on this passing.
Know you will always be here in our hearts
where you have written your name in love and caring.
You were the calm one, the logical one,
my anchor and my family.
We feel despair for those who tread this earth without those ties.
Ties made of memories and promises,
invisible yet unalterable between us.
No time or distance ever changed that between us.

Like the ebb and flow of the tides
our closeness and separateness
drifted through the years but at a second's notice
all markers were in place, all bonds reinforced,
the gap closed as if it never existed.
It did not really exist, only in the observance of others,
never in our hearts or souls, never in our love or relationship.

Time can seem like a jumble of episodes that have no order
and no value to anyone but those that share the bonds.
Our bond will not be broken, our bridge never burned,
the path will always be clear
and the seats on the bench we share together
free of dust and disrepair.

I want to bid you safe passage,
God speed and yet my selfish heart grasps to keep you—
but I love you more than that.
When you are ready, go, darlin',
go to those that have long waited to greet you again.
Go join the land where our dreams begin and I will see you there.
Save me a place…

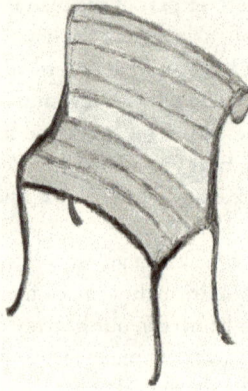

HAPPY BIRTHDAY, DEAR SISTER

I have no gift for you this year but me.
Whatever value you place on me is assigned worth only by you.
A culmination of years of cops and robbers, pirate ships and cap pistols.
Years of watching you fix your hair and sew your clothes.
Years sharing the same room, the same bed,
"Can you feel it now?" Mom would ask as we vied
for whatever breeze the fan slanted down on us
through the venetian blind.
We were typical female siblings a few years apart,
Dress-up times and cat fights;
walking to school and not wanting to be seen together.
Our childhood was normal as childhoods go.
We lived "without" some would say
but we lived with Michigan card games on the floor,
walks in a neighborhood long ago safe;
treats like sliced apples in front of the TV
and store-bought pastries on payday.
Memories of finding ways to occupy us all.
Marble games on the floor, our brother's electric train
beaming its tiny headlamp into the darkened room,
thunderstorms on the front porch,
fireworks at the beach from our own living room window,
not exactly living "without" I'd say.
Teenage years spent on opposite sides of the age fence,
a fence that finally came down when you went away to school.
Beginning appreciation of each other,
beginning relationship with each other,
totally apart from the past.

A new era of our sisterhood,
years of separation as each of us grew older,
lives moving separately yet in tandem,
still attached to the house we called home.
Life taught us many lessons,
some surrounded with blessed memories,
some with pangs of anguish.
Yet we survived it all and slipped into the future,
altering our paths and juggling our responsibilities
and changing our beliefs.
Each of us reaching a place, I believe,
where happiness and peace outweigh the rigors of everyday existence.
Because we are two distinct individuals
we will never read our past exactly the same,
but I'm so glad I get to ramble with you
about memories of events and people long past
yet deeply a part of our fabric.
We have woven a lovely fabric over the years,
a few dropped stitches, a few new designs;
our indefinable signature of a relationship
that began based in blood and grew into love.
You are my sister and,
according to the "sage wisdom" of our dear brother,
you don't have to love me but I know you do,
I hope you never stop as I love you.
There are so many things we share
that have produced the characters we inhabit now.
I would write our story the same again,
with you still my sister and also my friend.

A CANVAS

Do unto others as they do unto you
or before they do unto you.
That seems to be the philosophy
clouding our current society's vision.
Where did it come from, what shaped it
and how did it get so warped out of its true shape?
Look around and see with another's eyes
what the world may look like, smell, taste and feel.
Each pair of eyes sees a different picture
no matter what they are all looking at.
To color the book of life
in soothing shades and rays of hope,
one would need a palette supplied by the gods
or God, however you see it.
The paint smears and runs down the scene
on this canvas we call earth.
Seldom does it retain its original design,
one of beauty and glorious colors
beyond our imaginations.
We see what we want to see or believe that we see,
shaded by events and personalities
that influence our very breath.
Oh but to be able to breathe deep
and run freely across the face of this earth
is something that will not occur for many years.
We have so much to put back and renew.
So much that we have erased or eradicated;
so much that we lose each moment that passes.
Biding its time the earth waits for its window
for rebirth and the opportunity to give another species
the opportunity to start with a slate, not blank,
but dazzling with the hidden reality of nature,
long covered by our impudent strokes.
Wait, it is a true shame that we will not get to see...

THE QUEST

Brush to paper, charcoal to tablet,
spreading vermillion oil paint on a canvas
to portray the shades of a field.
What behooves anyone to do that?
What does it fulfill,
what does it empty out of the well
of each artist or expressionist?
Since we see the world through
so many different eyes and colors,
so many different tones and emotions,
that question has no single answer.
It lies within each artist and the relief or angst
that dwells in his mind or soul.
Nature started it really,
by painting the landscapes that spread before our eyes.
Nature colored the sky in daylight
to make us believe it might be touched or replicated
and showed the twinkling of stars
in the mist of the night to pique our curiosity.
The curiosity to see if one can reproduce either color or image
and trap it for all eternity.
It is a game she plays with us and we partake willingly.
Our childish attempts at beating her at her own game
most likely oft cause her to titter with laughter
or in very rare cases to catch her own breath
when one of us actually comes so close to matching her.
The freedom of mind and spirit
to chase this trail of pictures and shapes and creations
feeds many a soul and lifts up many a heart.
These images cause us to catch our breath
or feel our skin crawl or perhaps bumple our body with goose pimples.
What is it about these visages that cause such reactions,
such overwhelming needs to produce them?
Once again a question with no answer, a quest with no relief.

MEND

Where does one go from here.
How does rationale enter back into the picture.
A baby ready to join life takes its exit instead.
What can the lesson be,
Where exists the purpose behind
what shadow or lack of light
crept in over the soul to decide not to enter.
Leave before you even come.
Give others birth to dreams and visions that end in blackness.
Will this soul come again?
Will the bearer bear up again to make the journey.
Does the soul exist in another spirit
that will join with their path?
The fear to try again,
the assuredness to hold one already here and in need.
Let that idea possibly sprout and come to fruition.
There is a mending,
there is a continuation of the journey
once past the desolation.

JUDGEMENT

Judge not lest ye be judged.
Whether we realize it or not, judging happens
with almost every breath we take,
certainly with every thought that careens
through our minds.
Even the thought not to judge
is in a sense a judgement of how
we look at things around us.
We are created as a blank slate they say,
but with genetic tendencies towards various precepts.
We will be blonde, blue-eyed; auburn, green-eyed, etc.
Our eyes behold visions reflected and refracted
in them up on the screen in our brain.
Some things are gut-oriented in how we react or respond;
most others are taught, drilled or beaten into us
from infancy on.
We must be on constant vigilance if we were to try
to overcome judging even in the most miniscule fashion.
So much of our thoughts, words and interactions
become almost involuntary and we fall into that
"trap" because it takes less thought, less brainpower.
What would it be like to look at everything anew,
fresh eyes, blank filters on our consciousness?
Try it, if only for a moment.
I bet if you timed yourself
it would not even come close to lasting that long
The ability to look at something without judging it.
They say we use such a small portion of our actual brain;
isn't it a shame that so much RAM is actually taken up
with pre-established guidelines and identity factors?

www.ingramcontent.com/pod-product-compliance
Lightning Source LLC
Chambersburg PA
CBHW031332040426
42443CB00005B/305